3 MILES AN HOUR

HOW TO LET YOUR PACE
BE DETERMINED BY HIS SPIRIT

JONAH LUSK

3 Miles An Hour
Copyright © 2023 by Jonah Lusk

Scripture quotations taken from The Holy Bible, New International Version®, NIV®
Copyright © 1973, 1978, 1984, 2011 by Biblica, Inc.®
Used by permission. All rights reserved worldwide.

Scripture quotations marked NLT are taken from the Holy Bible, New Living Translation, copyright © 1996, 2004, 2015 by Tyndale House Foundation.
 Used by permission of Tyndale House Publishers, Inc., Carol Stream, Illinois 60188. All rights reserved.

All rights reserved. No part of this book may be reproduced or transmitted in any form or by any means, electronic, mechanical, photocopying, recording, or otherwise, without prior permission of the author.

Also by Jonah Lusk

Make Good Tables: Work. Family. Rest. And why God cares about more than just Sunday.

Covered In Dust: Rediscovering what it means to follow Jesus.

"God never hurries. There are no deadlines against which He must work. Only to know this is to quiet our spirits and relax our nerves."

A.W. Tozer

On the run

Do you like to run?

No? Me either.

But if you do like to run, that's fine.

Keep going.

I'll just sip my coffee everyday as you pass by.

Running is hard.

It's draining.

It's depleting.

I'm ok to just walk.

But if I'm honest, I've been running my whole life. Running to work. To games. To family gatherings. To church. To the bed to crash into a deep sleep.

Running is somehow a part of our DNA as humans.

Think back to the Garden of Eden.

You know the story.

Adam and Eve partake of the fruit from the tree God said was off limits.

They fall.

And then what do they do?

They run.

In their guilt and shame they run to hide.

And from that moment on, humanity has been in a constant state of running.

Always on. Always going. No time to stop. Trying everyday to cram it all in.

And the question is: *why?*

Why do we feel the need to run? To always be going?

To live our lives at an unsustainable pace?

In short, because it's a part of our sin nature.

We never feel good enough. We never feel like we have done enough. We have to try and do one more thing, just to prove to ourselves that we can actually do it on our own.

But the truth is: *we can't*.

We all have limits.

Limits that were given to us by God as a gift to embrace and not a burden to cast off.

At the beginning of creation, God gave the first human beings limits.

> *"You are free to eat from any tree in the garden; but you must not eat from the tree of the knowledge of good and evil, for when you eat from it you will certainly die."*
> (Genesis 2:16 NIV)

Every other tree in the garden was theirs to partake from.

Every other tree in the garden but one.

And the serpent comes in and tempts them to go beyond their limits because God has to be keeping something from them, right?

Well, no.

But they aren't ok to stay within their limits, so they eat from the one tree God commanded them not to partake of.

And the same thing happens to us each and every day.

All of us at some point in our lives have been tempted to push past our limits. To do more than we had the capacity or the energy to do, because we tend to believe that limits limit us.

But limits don't actually limit us.

They set us free.

When God gave Adam and Eve limits, He was not just trying to keep them from something. He was keeping them for something.

God wanted to keep them from being enslaved to the idea that nothing would ever be good enough.

God wanted to keep them for an abundant life that they never could have dreamed of.

See, at our core, we all know we have limits.

But the temptation is to constantly press past our limits because we think that what we really need is somewhere out "there."

You know what I mean, right?

That job. That title. That salary. That home. That trip.

Or maybe it's in your relationship with Jesus.

Somewhere out ahead of us is God, waving His arms at us, telling us His goodness and love and abundant life are out in front of us.

But it always seems to be just out of reach.

So we keep going. We keep running. We keep trying to do it all.

And we never really make any progress.

But what we need to know is that God's goodness and love and peace and joy are not somewhere out "there" ahead of us. They are behind us.

Chasing Us Down

Psalm 23 is a well-known passage of the Bible, and one many of you could quote from memory.

The entire passage is full of absolute gold, but I wanted to hone in on one specific verse.

Psalm 23:6 NLT:

> *"Surely Your goodness and unfailing love will pursue me all the days of my life, and I will live in the house of the LORD forever."*

What does the scripture say is pursuing us?

Goodness and unfailing love.

And notice the scripture tells us that God's goodness and unfailing love "pursue" us.

If they have to pursue us, could it be because we are always on the run?

And God's goodness and unfailing love are trying to catch us.

But if this is what scripture says is pursuing us, then why do we choose to run?

Why do we choose to live at an unsustainable pace of life?

It may be because we have believed the lie that God's goodness and His unfailing love are somewhere out "there," and that we have to pursue them.

And if God's goodness and mercy and unfailing love are way ahead of us, that must mean that something else is behind us.

Maybe it's our fears. Our worries. Our doubts. Our past. Our failures.

So we run and we strive.

And we try to do it all, as fast as we can, because deep inside we wonder whether or not we will ever catch up to God's goodness and His best for our life.

So, we spend our lives running. Which, as a result, leads to a life of exhaustion and burnout.

That's the bad news.

But here's the good news: Jesus also has a pace of life.

And His pace of life is completely counter to our culture.

See, when you read scripture, and you look at the life of Jesus, you never see Him in a hurry.

You never see Him running from town to town to preach His next sermon.

You never see Him overlooking people.

You never see Him frantic, or impatient.

You never see Jesus too busy to stop for the one.

No, when you look at how Jesus lived His life, you see Jesus walking.

You see Jesus talking to others, and taking the time to set a child on His lap.

You see Jesus looking up in a tree to lock eyes with an empty and broken man named Zacchaeus.

You see Jesus stopping to look up at the sky as the birds fly carefree.

See, Jesus had His own pace of life.

And it's important that we see Jesus and His pace of life correctly.

A.W. Tozer wisely said:

> *"What comes into our minds when we think about God is the most important thing about us."*

What comes into our minds when we think about Jesus directly influences our way of life.

So, if we believe Jesus is a busy God, with a lot to handle, and not a lot of time to get it all done, that's the life we will live.

If we see Jesus with a long to-do list for our lives, we will live our lives hurried and frantic, just trying to cram it all in.

But if we see Jesus as He truly is, as revealed in scripture, we will live our lives unhurried, at peace, and free.

So what do we do?

Maybe you're like me, and you have lived your life at an unsustainable pace for so long that it's become normal.

Maybe you're like me, and your fast pace of life is slowly crushing your soul, as you sprint through your days, trying to do it all.

What's the answer?

How can we begin to live at a sustainable pace of life?

A life where we take time to look up at the sky.

A life where we stop for the person in the hallway at work because we aren't in a hurry anymore.

A life where we aren't frantic, but at peace.

This is the life that Jesus invites us into.

The Pace of Love

Did you know the average walking pace of an adult is three miles an hour?[1]

And when you think about the life of Jesus, lived in a culture without planes or trains, walking was a integral part of His daily life.

So Jesus, the visible image of the invisible God, had a pace that He walked at. And that pace was more than likely three miles an hour.

Japanese theologian Kosuke Koyama said:

> "God walks slowly because he is love. If he is not love he would have gone much faster. Love has its speed. It is a spiritual speed. It is a different kind of speed from the technological speed to which we are accustomed. It goes on in the depth of our life, whether we notice it or not, at three miles an hour. It is the speed we walk and therefore the speed the love of God walks."[2]

Our God has a pace.

And it's the pace of love.

Unhurried. Peaceful. Present.

It's different, yet it's familiar.

It's ancient, yet it's our future.

To walk eternally at the pace of love.

To walk at a pace of three miles an hour.

So let's begin.

"There is no greater need today than the freedom to lay down the heavy burden of getting ahead."

Richard Foster

Be honest

Let's take a look at a familiar scripture:

> "God blesses those who are poor (in spirit) and realize their need for Him, for the Kingdom of Heaven is theirs."
> *(Matthew 5:3 NLT)*

It's interesting that the word for poor in this scripture means "helpless and powerless to accomplish an end." [3]

I believe a lot of us struggle to slow our pace of life down because, at our core, we believe that we can accomplish it all. We believe that we can do it all.

Or, maybe we believe that we have to do it all.

Either way, the truth is: *we can't*.

We can't do it all.

We are all helpless and powerless to accomplish whatever end we desire, because we all have limits.

We all have boundaries and limitations in our lives that are a gift from God.

And these boundaries are what you might call being human.

And if we want to live at the peaceful, sustainable pace of Jesus, we have to begin with being honest that we can't do it all.

We can't be everywhere, all the time.

We can't fill our schedules with everyone else's agenda, and expect to live a healthy, joyful life.

We have to be honest with ourselves that we are human, and we have limits.

And not just that we have limits, but that we can't do it on our own.

We have to be honest with ourselves that we are fully dependent on God.

Remember Jesus' teaching on the vine and the branches in John 15?

What did Jesus say regarding Himself as the vine, and us as the branches?

> "Remain in me, as I also remain in you. No branch can bear fruit by itself; it must remain in the vine. Neither can you bear fruit unless you remain in me." (John 15:4 NIV)

Jesus is very clear.

A branch cannot bear fruit by itself.

It must stay connected to the vine.

Jesus later states it even more clearly when He says:

> "...apart from Me you can do nothing." (John 15:5 NIV)

By ourselves, and on our own, we are helpless, powerless, and fruitless.

But when we choose to remain connected to the vine, fruit can be produced in our lives.

When we choose to be honest that we can't do it all, and that we can't do it by ourselves, we choose to freely abide in Jesus.

And when we abide in Jesus, Jesus begins to produce things in us and through us that we could have never dreamed of.

So if we want to begin living like Jesus, we have to first be honest with ourselves that we can't do it all, and that we can't do it on our own.

Practice

To practice the first step of being honest, we have to set aside time to simply abide in, and be with, Jesus.

And this will look differently depending on your season of life.

This might look like an early morning on the porch with your coffee.

Or maybe it's your drive into work after you drop the kids off at school.

Regardless of the time or place, set aside time to be with Jesus and express your dependence on Him.

You can even engage in this practice with your body by taking deep breaths in and out, as you visualize yourself sitting at His feet, or leaning on His chest.

And remember: the goal is to simply be with Jesus and spend time in His presence.

Because it's in being with Jesus that we become free to be honest about our limits, so we can embrace His power and His strength for our lives.

Embracing our limits is what opens us to embrace God's strength and power.

We are finite.

He is infinite.

And at the end of the day, the truth still remains: we need Jesus.

Without Him, apart from Him, we can do nothing.

And in order for us to begin living at His pace for our lives, we have to be honest with ourselves that we do in fact need Him.

So take a moment today, maybe a 30 second window before walking through the front door of your home after work, and do these 3 things:

Embrace your limits.
Express your dependence.
Receive His grace.

And then, walk with Him.

Let Him show you a new way to carry the load.

Let Him reveal to you a new way to live.

"You have to decide what your highest priorities are and have the courage pleasantly, smilingly, and non-apologetically - to say no to other things. And the way to do that is by having a bigger yes burning inside."

Stephen Covey

Say no

The one word, in my opinion, that might carry more power than any other word in the English language is simply this:

No.

This one word has the potential to free you from the burden of other people's expectations and agendas.

This tiny word has the power to create margin and space in your life, in order to help you slow down and live at peace.

And here's the best part: Jesus said no.

Let's allow the Gospel of Mark to set the stage.

> "Very early in the morning, while it was still dark, Jesus got up, left the house and went off to a solitary place, where He prayed. Simon and his companions went to look for Him, and when they found Him, they exclaimed: 'Everyone is looking for you!'" (Mark 1:35-37 NIV)

Jesus has ministered all day prior. He's healed the sick. Restored the broken. Set the captive free.

Needless to say, it was a full day.

And early the next morning, Jesus gets up while everyone else is still asleep, and He finds a solitary place to pray.

Later, Simon and the other disciples awake to find Jesus missing, and so they began the search.

Upon finding Jesus, they seem a little puzzled by Jesus' actions, and frustrated that He would leave crowds of people to go off on His own to pray.

"Everyone is looking for you!" (Mark 1:38 NIV)

Translation: Everyone has their own idea of what You need to do and where You need to go and how much You should be doing today Jesus.

And sadly, everyone does have their own agenda for Jesus.

And everyone also has their own agenda for your life.

Where you should go.

What you should do.

What degree you should get.

What car to drive.

You know what I mean, right?

Most of us live with this weight on our shoulders that can usually be attributed to the plans, agendas, and expectations of other people.

And Jesus was not exempt from this weight.

But in this moment, Jesus is simply taking some time to sit with His Father, and just be.

But here come the disciples carrying with them their own expectations, as well as the expectations of the people they have been ministering to.

And look at how Jesus responds:

> "Jesus replied, 'Let us go somewhere else - to the nearby villages - so I can preach there also. That is why I have come.'" (Mark 1:39 NIV)

Translation: No.

What was Jesus saying to Simon and the disciples and all of the people in the town?

"No."

"But everyone is looking for You, Jesus!"

"No."

"But everyone wanted You to do that healing thing today, and maybe that bread thing tomorrow."

"No."

What was Jesus saying?

Jesus was saying no.

But, let's not stop there.

Jesus was also saying yes.

No to staying here, yes to going there.

No to their agenda, yes to His Father's agenda.

Jesus was saying "no to this, yes to that."

See, your yes to one thing speaks a no to another thing.

And let's think about it for a minute.

What are you saying no to right now because of your yes?

Yes to another activity might be a no to a meal together at the table this evening.

Yes to late hours at my job might be a no to a day of rest with my family.

Yes to everyone else's agenda for your life might be a no to God's calling and purpose for your life.

See, your yes to one thing is a no to something else.
Which means we have to use wisdom in what we say "yes" to, and what we say "no" to.

And the scripture reveals to us how Jesus was able to say no.

> "'Let us go somewhere else - to the nearby villages - so I can preach there also. That is **why** I have come.'"
> (Mark 1:39 NIV, emphasis mine)

Jesus said no because He had a why.

Jesus tells His disciples, "I'm saying no because I know why I have come."

Because Jesus knew why He was on the earth, and what His purpose was in life, He was empowered to say no to what might take away from who He was called to be and what He was called to do.

So, ask yourself: *What is my why?*

I recently became a parent, so for me, my son is my why.

My son is my yes.

Which means it's a no to late hours at work.

It's a yes to a day of rest each week with my family, so it's a no to the other things we might be invited to on that day.

Because I know my why, I know what is a clear yes, and what is a clear no.

Your why in life will empower you to say no to the things that hinder you from walking in the life God created for you to walk in.

Jesus said no.

So it's ok for you to say no, too.

Practice

I'll be honest, no is an easy word, but it's not an easy word to say.

So, to practice, choose one thing over the next week to say no to.

Maybe it's another lunch out with your coworkers, so you can take that lunch hour to breathe and regather your thoughts.

Maybe it's that third birthday party you were invited to next weekend, because somehow every child was born within the same week.

Maybe it's that second or third episode of your favorite series tonight, so you can read a book with your children.

Regardless of what it is, just practice saying no.

And remember, you're not just saying no.

You're saying yes to something more important and more valuable.

You're saying yes to your why in life, and no to what doesn't align with your why.

And I promise, saying no will set you free.

"It is good to have an end to journey toward; but it is the journey that matters in the end."

Ernest Hemingway

Play the long game

Here's one of the most important questions you can ask yourself: *Who am I becoming?*

You can also put it in the context of your family by asking: *Who are we becoming?*

See, you have to play the long game with your life and with your family and with your job.

The question is not just "what do we have to do this week?"

A more important question to ask is: *Who are we becoming?* Because Jesus is more interested in who we are becoming than where we are going.

Jesus is more interested in who we are becoming on the journey than where the journey takes us.

But for the most part, our focus is on where we are going and what we are doing.

But scripture tells us something different.

> "For God knew His people in advance, and He chose them to **become** like His Son, so that His Son would be the firstborn among many brothers and sisters." (Romans 8:29 NLT, emphasis mine).

See, God's heart for us as His sons and daughters is to become like Jesus.

So I want you to ask yourself: *Who am I becoming?*

And let's be honest, a lot of us don't want to take the time to answer that question because it's easier to run from thing to thing to thing as fast as we can than it is to slow down and listen to what God wants to say to us.

I know we have hectic days.

That's just a part of life.

It's almost a prerequisite for living.

But the danger is that a hectic day turns into a hectic week. And that hectic week turns into a hectic month, which turns into a hectic year.

And before you know it, you've lived a hectic life because sprinting and running became normal.

So, maybe you've been asking yourself: *Where am I going? What am I doing?*

But Jesus might be asking you the question: *Who are you becoming?*

Jesus might be asking: *Who is your family becoming?*

Take a moment to ask yourself: *Is my pace of life making me more tired and more frustrated and more anxious?*

Or, am I becoming more loving and more patient and more kind and more intentional?

Because God's heart is for us to become like His Son Jesus.

And what type of life did Jesus lead?

Did He live a life of hurry and doubt and worry and fear and exhaustion?

Or was Jesus a person of love and joy and peace?

See, how we see Jesus is how we will represent Him.

How we see Jesus is how our family will represent Him.

Will my family be burned out, worn down, and exhausted? Or will we live with peace and joy?

When my kids are grown, will they run frantically through their lives?

Or, will they have a value for sitting down with their family to eat in the evening, just like we did as they grew up?

Will my children live their lives saying yes to everything, or will they know how to say no?

In 40 years, will I be more anxious and bitter and tired?

Or, will I be more loving and more peaceful and more like Jesus?

The question for our lives is not: *Where am I going, and what am I doing?*

The better question for our lives is: *Am I becoming more or less like Jesus?*

Because Jesus didn't live a life of speed and hurry and anxiety.

Jesus took time for the prostitute broken at His feet.

Jesus took time for the woman in a crowd with the issue of blood.

Jesus took time to weep at the tomb of Lazarus.

And wherever Jesus went, He brought healing and peace and hope and life.

That's who I want to be.

And with God's grace, day by day, that's who I am becoming.

Practice

For our last practice, there are two components.

First, we **repent**.

Then, we choose to **keep in step with the Spirit**.

Let me touch on both.

Our first step to playing the long game is to **repent**.

Yes, repentance seems like an old church word that carries some negative connotations, but its meaning goes far deeper than walking down the aisle at church.

In Acts 3, the Apostle Peter is preaching to a crowd of people, who ask the question: *what do we do?*

And Peter responds by saying:

> "Repent, then, and turn to God, so that your sins may be wiped out, that times of **refreshing** may come from the Lord." (Acts 3:19 NIV, emphasis mine).

What does repentance do?

It brings refreshing.

The word for refreshing here in Greek is *anapsyxis*, which means "a cooling, refreshing, a recovery of breath."[4]

When we repent, we recover our breath.

And remember what the Lord does in Psalm 23?

> "He refreshes my soul." (Psalm 23:3 NIV)

When we repent, and say 'Jesus, I am living at an unsustainable pace that is not from You, and it's a pace that I can't sustain. And I repent for trying to go beyond my limits,' we receive refreshing and we recover our breath.

And I don't know about you, but I need to recover my breath.

After we repent, the next step to playing the long game is to **keep in step with the Spirit.**

The Apostle Paul, writing to the Galatians, states:

> "Since we live by the Spirit, let us keep in step with the Spirit." (Galatians 5:25 NIV)

Notice Paul didn't say to "keep up with the Spirit."

Or to "run frantically with the Spirit."

See, we have to make a decision to let our pace be determined by the Spirit.

We cannot allow our pace of life to be determined by culture or by friends or by social media or by news.

When the culture around us says to run and do and cram it all in, the Spirit speaks tenderly to us to slow down, trust, and rest.

We have to allow the pace of our life and the life of our families to be determined by the Spirit.

Because it's not anxiety and worry and fear and failure that are pursuing us.

God's goodness and His love are not somewhere out "there" that we have to run around trying to find.

No, His love and His mercy and His forgiveness and His peace are pursuing us all the days of our lives.

So what if we stopped running and let them catch us?

Endnotes

1) Hullett, A. (2020, March 9). Let's Talk the Walk: How Does Your Walking Speed Stack Up Against the Average? Greatist. https://greatist.com/health/average-walking-speed

2) Koyama, K. (1980). Three Mile an Hour God: Biblical Reflections. Orbis Books.

3) G4434 - ptōchos - Strong's Greek Lexicon (nlt). (n.d.). Blue Letter Bible. https://www.blueletterbible.org/lexicon/g4434/nlt/mgnt/0-1/

4) G403 - anapsyxis - Strong's Greek Lexicon (nlt). (n.d.). Blue Letter Bible. https://www.blueletterbible.org/lexicon/g403/nlt/mgnt/0-1/

Thank you for reading!

I plan to release more books just like this in the future.

If you'd like to get them sent to your inbox, subscribe at <u>jonahlusk.com</u>

Made in the USA
Middletown, DE
01 February 2025